THAT NEW WORLD,

AND

OTHER POEMS.

BY

MRS. S. M. B. PIATT,

AUTHOR OF "A WOMAN'S POEMS," "A VOYAGE TO THE FORTUNATE ISLES, ETC."

BOSTON:

JAMES R. OSGOOD AND COMPANY.

(Late Ticknor & Fields, and Fields, Osgood, & Co.)

1877.

The Riverside Press, Cambridge:
STEREOTYPED AND PRINTED BY
H. O. HOUGHTON AND COMPANY.

CONTENTS.

THAT NEW WORLD, Etc.

OTHER POEMS.

WITH CHILDREN.

THAT NEW WORLD, ETC.

THAT NEW WORLD.

How gracious we are to grant to the dead
  Those wide, vague lands in the foreign sky,
Reserving this world for ourselves instead —
  For we must live, though others must die!

And what is this world that we keep, I pray?
  True, it has glimpses of dews and flowers;
Then Youth and Love are here and away,
  Like mated birds — but nothing is ours.

Ah, nothing indeed, but we cling to it all.
  It is nothing to hear one's own heart beat,
It is nothing to see one's own tears fall;
  Yet surely the breath of our life is sweet.

Yes, the breath of our life is so sweet, I fear
  We were loath to give it for all we know
Of that charméd Country we hold so dear,
  Far into whose beauty the breathless go.

Yet certain we are, when we see them fade
  Out of the pleasant light of the sun,
Of the sands of gold in the palm-leaf's shade,
  And the strange, high jewels all these have
      won.

You dare not doubt it, O soul of mine!
  And yet, if these empty eyes could see
One, only one, from that voyage divine,
  With something, anything, sure for me!

Ah, blow me the scent of one lily, to tell
  That it grew outside of this world, at most;
Ah, show me a plume to touch, or a shell
  That whispers of some unearthly coast!

ENCHANTED.

SHE sat in a piteous hut
  In a wood where poisons grew;
Withered was every leaf,
  And her face was withered too.
Like a sword the fierce wind cut
  Her worn heart through and through.

Gray as the frost was her hair,
  Dim as the dusk were her eyes,
As still as stone was her mouth;
  Yet she knew that she was fair,
And she knew that she was wise.
  Therefore she waited there.

Away, and so far away,
  She looked for a light and a sign:
"Oh, he has not forgotten me!
  What should I care for to-day,
When all to-morrow is mine?
  I am content to stay."

On the heights the hail would beat,
  In the thorns would sink the snow,
And the chasms were weird with sound;
  Yet the years would come and go:
"Somewhere there is something sweet,
  And sometime I shall know.

"There is a land close by,
  A land in reach of my arm;
It is mine from shore to sea; —
  There the nightingales do fly,
There the flush of the rose is warm:
  I shall take it by and by.

"But the shape that guards the gate,
  Where my mirror waits to show
How beautiful I am,
  Oh, he makes me loath to go.
I wait, and I wait, and I wait, —
  Through fear of him, I know.

"But who breaks this charm of breath
  Enchantment himself must wear.
Two from each other shrink
  In the freezing dark, and stare: . . . .
Your kiss for my kiss, O Death!
  Each makes the other fair."

THE ALTAR AT ATHENS.

"TO THE UNKNOWN GOD."

BECAUSE my life was hollow with a pain
  As old as — death: because my eyes were dry
As the fierce tropics after months of rain:
  Because my restless voice said "Why?" and "Why?"

Wounded and worn, I knelt within the night,
  As blind as darkness — Praying? And to Whom? —
When yon cold crescent cut my folded sight,
  And showed a phantom Altar in my room.

It was the Altar Paul at Athens saw.
The Greek bowed there, but not the Greek alone;
The ghosts of nations gathered, wan with awe,
And laid their offerings on that shadowy stone.

The Egyptian worshiped there the crocodile,
There they of Nineveh the bull with wings;
The Persian there, with swart sun-lifted smile,
Felt in his soul the writhing fire's bright stings.

There the weird Druid held his mistletoe;
There for the scorched son of the sand, coiled bright,
The torrid snake was hissing sharp and low;
And there the Western savage paid his rite.

"Allah!" the Moslem darkly muttered there;
"Brahma!" the jeweled Indies of the East
Sighed through their spices, with a languid
prayer;
"Christ?" faintly questioned many a paler
priest.

And still the Athenian Altar's glimmering
Doubt
On all religions — evermore the same.
What tears shall wash its sad inscription out?
What Hand shall write thereon His other
name?

LADY FRANKLIN.

In shadowy ships, that freeze,
We think of men who sail, the frozen-fated;
Tears, if you will, for these.
But oh, the truest searcher of the seas
In the blown breath of English daisies waited.

. . . . A Pathway, here or there,
He sought — the old, unlighted Pathway finding:
Out of the North's despair,
Out of the South's flower-burdened wastes of air,
To that great Peaceful Sea forever winding.

. . . . Oh, after *her* vague quest
  Among weird winds, in icy deserts, lonely,
Has she laid down to rest
Under a Palm, whose light leaves on her
    breast
  Drop balms of summer, sun and silence
    only?

Has some one whispered: "Why,
  O woman faithful, why this dark delaying
Outside the pleasant sky?—
How could you seek me in the snows, when I
  Here, in the Loveliest Land of all, was
    staying?"

HER CROSS AND MINE.

"THIS is my cross — here, Sister, see:
  The only one I have to bear."
A flash of gold fell over me,
  And precious lights were everywhere.

She was a lovely, restless thing,
  With time in blossom at her feet,
And on her hand the enchanted ring
  Whose promise always is so sweet.

I was a nun. My fearless eyes
  Had looked their last on youth. I guessed
At something quiet in the skies,
  And veiled my face against the rest.

My cross was dark and darkly stained,
  Even from the heart of one who died :—
Invisible drops of blood had rained
  Thereon, when love was crucified.

That laughing girl could pity me,
  Because she fancied from my cross
The world had fallen. Such as she
  Still think to lose the world — is loss!

Yet, heavier is her cross than mine,
  For in the fatal jewels there
(Oh, will she ask for help divine?)
  I know she has the world to bear.

COUNTING THE GRAVES.

"How many graves are in this world?" "Oh, child,"
His mother answered, "surely there are two."
Archly he shook his pretty head and smiled:
"I mean in this whole world, you know I do!"

"Well, then, in this whole world: in East and West,
In North and South, in dew and sand and snow,
In all sad places where the dead may rest:
There are two graves — yes, there are two, I know."

"But graves have been here for a thousand
years, —
Or, for ten thousand? Soldiers die, and
kings;
And Christians die — sometimes." "My own
poor tears
Have never yet been troubled by these
things.

. . . . "More graves within the hollow
ground, in sooth,
Than there are stars in all the pleasant
sky? —
Where did you ever learn such dreary truth,
Oh, wiser and less selfish far than I?

"I did not know, — I who had light and breath:
Something to touch, to look at, if no more.
Fair earth to live in, who believe in death,
Till, dumb and blind, he lies at their own
door?"

. . . . "I did not know — I may have heard or
read —
Of more; but should I search the wide
grass through,
Lift every flower and every thorn," she said,
"From every grave — oh, I should see but
two!"

IN HER PRISON.

WATCHED with the cruel watching of the stars
Barred by the powers of darkness with their
bars :

Oh ! those that see me see as far as space,
And these that hold me circle every place.

My feet are tangled in the chains of Time,
My hands cannot take hold on air and climb.

And I am dumb — because the heavens are
high,
And who can hope to scale them with a cry ?

The floor is gray with mould on which I tread,
Dust gathers in the silence overhead.

With bitter bread and water hardly sweet
My jailer mocks me, saying : " Drink and eat."

Yet somewhere there are carpets soft and rare,
And lights and laughter in the world — some-
where ?

And somewhere there are golden cups of wine,
And snowy cakes where combs of honey shine.

Through other lips I taste the wine, and touch
Through other feet the carpets — that is much.

I see through other eyes the lights, and hear
The laughter clearly, not with mine own ear.

My grating gathers me a drop of dew ;
Some piteous blossom sends its sweetness
through.

Some tender bird, far on a sunny tree,
Breaks his wild song and gives one half to me.

The palace music leaves the palace guest,
And falls to dreaming here upon my breast.

Yet, spite of all, sometimes my Prison shakes
With the great yearning of a heart that aches.

Oh! that its lonesome roof would fall to-night,
And show me for an instant — something
White!

WE TWO.

God's will is — the bud of the rose for your
hair,
The ring for your hand and the pearl for
your breast;
God's will is — the mirror that makes you look
fair.
No wonder you whisper: "God's will is the
best."

But what if God's will were the famine, the
flood? —
And were God's will the coffin shut down in
your face? —
And were God's will the worm in the fold of
the bud,
Instead of the picture, the light, and the lace?

Were God's will the arrow that flieth by night,
  Were God's will the pestilence walking by day,
The clod in the valley, the rock on the height —
  I fancy "God's will" would be harder to say.

God's will is — your own will. What honor have you
  For having your own will, awake or asleep?
Who praises the lily for keeping the dew,
  When the dew is so sweet for the lily to keep?

God's will unto me is not music or wine.
  With helpless reproaching, with desolate tears,
God's will I resist, for God's will is divine;
  And I — shall be dust to the end of my years.

God's will is — not mine. Yet one night I
shall lie
Very still at his feet, where the stars may not
shine.
"Lo! I am well pleased," I shall hear from the
sky;
Because — it is God's will I do, and not mine.

THE GIFT OF EMPTY HANDS.

A FAIRY TALE.

THEY were two Princes doomed to death ;
Each loved his beauty and his breath :
" Leave us our life and we will bring
Fair gifts unto our lord, the King."

They went together. In the dew
A charméd bird before them flew.
Through sun and thorn one followed it ;
Upon the other's arm it lit.

A rose, whose faintest flush was worth
All buds that ever blew on earth,
One climbed the rocks to reach ; ah, well,
Into the other's breast it fell.

Weird jewels, such as fairies wear,
When moons go out, to light their hair,
One tried to touch on ghostly ground ;
Gems of quick fire the other found.

One with the dragon fought to gain
The enchanted fruit, and fought in vain ;
The other breathed the garden's air
And gathered precious apples there.

Backward to the imperial gate
One took his fortune, one his fate :
One showed sweet gifts from sweetest lands,
The other torn and empty hands.

At bird, and rose, and gem, and fruit,
The King was sad, the King was mute ;
At last he slowly said : "My son,
True treasure is not lightly won.

"Your brother's hands, wherein you see
Only these scars, show more to me
Than if a kingdom's price I found
In place of each forgotten wound."

A QUEEN AT HOME.

THEY know that the world is mine,
  (I am but a name to them,)
And they fancy its jewels shine
  All over my garment's hem.

My face seems bright from afar
  To their loyal eyes and trust:
But who looks too close at a star
  Will find it is made of dust.

My friend, you have whiter bread;
  My friend, you have redder wine,
And a fairer roof for your head,
  Though beggar you be, than mine.

To the poor I give of my gold;
  By the wounded I watch at night;
To the eyes of the dying I hold
  A cross — not mine own — for a light.

Yes, the world is mine, but I pray
  On my cloister floor alone;
My hood and my cloak are gray,
  And my pillow is but a stone.

ANSWERING A CHILD.

But if I should ask the king? —
He could if he would? Ah, no.
Though he took from his hand the ring,
Though he took from his head the crown —
In the dust I should lay them down.

If I sat at a fairy's feet? —
A fairy could if she would?
(Oh, the fairy-faith is sweet!)
Though she gave me her wand and her wings,
To me they were pitiful things.

Ask God? — He can if He will? —
He is better than fairies or kings?
(Ask God? — He would whisper: "Be still.")

Though He gave me each star I can see
Through my tears — it were nothing to me.

" He can do " ——— But He cannot undo
The terrible darkened gate
Which the fire of His will went through,
Leading the Dead away.
For the Past it is vain to pray !

THE KING'S MEMENTO MORI.

INTO the regal face the risen sun
  Laughed, and he whispered in dismay:
"How is it, Victor of a World, that none
  Remind you what you are, to-day?

"Your sword shall teach the slave, who could forget
  That men are mortal, what they are!
How dared he sleep, — he has not warned me yet, —
  After the last, loath, lagging star?"

. . . Across his palace threshold, wan and still,
  His morning herald, wet with dew,

Stared at him with fixed eyes that well might
chill
The vanity of earth all through.

"Good morrow, King," he heard the dead lips
say;
"See what is man. When did I tell
My bitter message to my lord, I pray,
So reverently and so well?"

MY BIRTHRIGHT.

If I was born the helpless heir,
  Ah me, to some vague foreign place,
Somewhere — and is it not somewhere? —
  In the weird loneliness of Space,
Why is my native grass so sweet,
And tangled so about my feet?

If I, without my will, must take
  Immortal gifts of pearl and gold,
And white saint-garments, for the sake
  Of my fair soul, why must I hold
The jewels of the dust so dear,
And purple and fine linen, here?

If One has been for love of mine
  Willing, unseen of me, to die —
A Prince whose beauty is divine,
  Whose kingdom without end — ah, why
Would I forsake his face and moan,
Only to kiss and keep your own?

If I, unworthy of my dower
  Among the palms of Paradise,
Would give it for a funeral flower
  (In folded hands, that need not rise),
Why may not some true angel be
Rich with estate too high for me?

COMFORT — BY A COFFIN.

Ah, friend of mine,
The old enchanted story! — Oh
I cannot hear a word!
Tell some poor child who loved a bird,
And knows he holds it stained and still,
" It flies — in Fairyland!
Its nest is in a palm-tree, on a hill;
Go, catch it — if you will!"

Ah, friend of mine,
The music (which ear hath not heard?)
At best wails from the skies,
Somehow, into our funeral cries!

The flowers (eye hath not seen?) still fail
To hide the coffin lid;
Against this face, so pitiless now and pale,
Can the high heavens avail?

Ah, friend of mine,
I think you mean — to mean it all!
But then an angel's wing
Is a remote and subtle thing,
(If you could show me any such
In air that I can breathe!)
And surely Death's cold hand has much, so much,
About it we can touch!

Ah, friend of mine,
Say nothing of the thorns — and then
Say nothing of the snow.
God's will? It is — that thorns must grow,

Despite our bare and troubled feet,
  To crown Christ on the cross;
The snow keeps white watch on the unrisen
    wheat,
  And yet — the world is sweet.

  Ah, friend of mine,
I know, I know — all you can know!
  All you can say is — this:
"It is the last time you can kiss
This only one of all the dead,
  Knowing it is the last;
These are the last tears you can ever shed
  On this fair fallen head."

SAD WISDOM — FOUR YEARS OLD.

"WELL, but some time I will be dead;
  Then you will love me, too!"
Ah! mouth so wise for mouth so red,
  I wonder how you knew.
(Closer, closer, little brown head —
  Not long can I keep you!)

Here, take this one poor bud to hold,
  Take this long kiss and last;
Love cannot loosen one fixed fold
  Of the shroud that holds you fast —
Never, never; oh, cold, so cold!
  All that was sweet is past.

Oh, tears, and tears, and foolish tears,
  Dropped on a grave somewhere!
Does not the child laugh in my ears
  What time I feign despair?
Whisper, whisper — I know he hears;
  Yet this is hard to bear.

O world, with your wet face above
  One veil of dust, thick-drawn!
O weird voice of the hapless dove,
  Broken for something gone!
Tell me, tell me, when will we love
  The thing the sun shines on?

GIVING UP THE WORLD.

So, from the ruins of the world alone
  Can Heaven be builded? Oh,
What other temples must be overthrown,
  Founded in sand or snow!

But, Heaven can not be built with jewelled hands?
  Then — from my own I wring
Glitter of gold, the gifts of many lands;
  The seas their pearls I fling.

Heaven must be hung with pictures of the dead?
  The shroud must robe the saint?
Never one halo round a living head
  Would Raphael dare to paint?

Heaven must have flowers — after the worm
has crossed
Their blush, the wind their breath ?
After the utter silence of the frost
Has made them white with death ?

Heaven must have music — but the birds that
sing
In that divinest nest
Thither must waver, wounded in the wing
And wounded in the breast ?

Heaven must be lighted — at the fallen light
Of moon, and star, and sun ?
Ah me ! since these have made the earth too
bright,
Let the dark Will be done !

NO HELP.

WHEN will the flowers grow there? I cannot
    tell.
  Oh, many and many a rain will beat there
    first,
Stormy and dreary, such as never fell
  Save when the heart was breaking that had
    nursed
Something most dear a little while, and then
Murmured at giving God his own again.

The woods were full of violets, I know;
  And some wild sweet-briers grew so near
    the place:
Their time is not yet come. Dead leaves and
    snow
  Must cover first the darling little face

From these wet eyes, forever fixed upon
Your last still cradle, O most precious one!

Is he not with his Father? So I trust.
  Is he not His? Was he not also mine?
His mother's empty arms yearn toward the
    dust.
  Heaven lies too high, the soul is too divine.
I wake at night and miss him from my breast,
And — human words can never say the rest.

Safe? But out of the world, out of my sight!
  My way to him through utter darkness lies.
I am gone blind with weeping, and the light —
  If there be light — is shut inside the skies.
Think you, to give my bosom back his breath,
I would not kiss him from the peace called
    Death?

And do I want a little Angel? No,
I want my Baby — with such piteous pain,
That were this bitter life thrice bitter, oh!
I could not choose but take him back again.
God cannot help me, for God cannot break
His own dark Law — for my poor sorrow's
sake.

HOME AGAIN.

It is a mournful thing to have no home,
To wear a shroud of loneliness on earth,
To know that fate has forced thee forth to roam,
And fear thyself unwelcome by each hearth,—
To hear harsh, stranger voices, and to raise
A drooping lid and meet a loveless gaze!

Once, long ago, the lightning's quivering glare
Lit the strange sadness of a boyish face,
And vanished from bright waves of tangled hair
That seemed to touch the dark with sunny grace,

While the sad wind with many a fond caress
Sighed for a kindred wanderer's loneliness.

Weary and wretched he had sunk to sleep
  Ere sunset's crimson loveliness was gone;
The twilight came and passed, night's gloom grew deep
  In the damp forest; still he slumbered on,
And — oh! how strange! — that friendless wanderer smiled
As calmly as a cradled, thoughtless child.

For Memory bore him to his home; he heard
  The murmured music of his childish hours,
He saw familiar trees and each bright bird
  Whose sweet song gushed at Spring-time mid the flowers;
His sister smiled, his mother's thrilling kiss
Flush'd his pale cheek with more than former bliss.

He woke, while listening to the words of love,
And heard the passing night-wind's deep farewell!
He saw the trees around, the clouds above,
And murmured, starting from that blessèd spell,
"O God! the loved are gone — my dream is o'er;
This is a forest — I 've a home no more!"

. . . World-wanderer, thou art in a forest too!
Oh! dream and smile as did that lonely boy:
There is a home for thee: the loved, the true,
Await thee there amid unfading joy;
Weary and sad thou too shalt fall asleep:
The shades around thee shall be dim and deep.

Angels shall bear thee to thy home, and thou
Shalt wake amid the light of early years;

Thy mother's real kiss shall thrill thy brow
And still the quivering of earth's lingering fears;
Remembered voices, with an added strain
Of trembling love, will whisper Home Again!

1857.

ASKING FOR TEARS.

OH, let me come to Thee in this wild way,
Fierce with a grief that will not sleep, to pray
Of all thy treasures, Father, only one,
After which I may say — Thy will be done.

Nay, fear not Thou to make my time too sweet.
I nurse a Sorrow, — kiss its hands and feet,
Call it all piteous, precious names, and try,
Awake at night, to hush its helpless cry.

The sand is at my moaning lip, the glare
Of the uplifted desert fills the air ;
My eyes are blind and burning, and the years
Stretch on before me. Therefore, give me Tears !

CALLING THE DEAD.

My little child, so sweet a voice might wake
So sweet a sleeper for so sweet a sake.
Calling your buried brother back to you,
You laugh and listen — till I listen too!

. . . . Why does he listen? It may be to hear
Sounds too divine to reach my troubled ear.
Why does he laugh? It may be he can see
The face that only tears can hide from me.

Poor baby faith — so foolish or so wise:
The name I shape out of forlornest cries
He speaks as with a bird's or blossom's breath.
How fair the knowledge is that knows not
Death!

. . . . Ah, fools and blind — through all the piteous years
Searchers of stars and graves — how many seers,
Calling the dead, and seeking for a sign,
Have laughed and listened, like this child of mine?

OTHER POEMS.

"FOLDED HANDS."

THE STORY OF A PICTURE.

MADONNA eyes looked at him from the air,
But never from the picture. Still he painted.
The hovering halo would not touch the hair,
The patient saint still stared at him — unsainted.

Day after day flashed by in flower and frost;
Night after night, how fast the stars kept burning
His little light away, till all was lost! —
All, save the bitter sweetness of his yearning.

Slowly he saw his work: it was not good.
Ah, hopeless hope! Ah, fiercely-dying passion!

"I am no painter," moaned he as he stood,
With folded hands in death's unconscious fashion.

"Stand as you are, an instant!" some one cried.
He felt the voice of a diviner brother.
The man who was a painter, at his side,
Showed how his folded hands could serve another.

Ah, strange, sad world, where Albert Dürer takes
The hands that Albert Dürer's friend has folded,
And with their helpless help such triumph makes! —
Strange, since both men of kindred dust were molded.

THE LONGEST DEATH-WATCH.*

THE woman is a picture now.
  The Spanish suns have touched her face ;
The coil of gold upon her brow
  Shines back on an Imperial race
  With most forlorn and bitter grace.

Old palace-lamps behind her burn,
  The ermine molders on her train.
Her ever-constant eyes still yearn
  For one who came not back to Spain ;
  And dim and hollow is her brain.

* Joanna, the wife of Philip the Handsome, was the daughter of Ferdinand and Isabella, sister of Catherine of Aragon, and mother of the Emperor Charles V.

One only thing she knew in life,
  Four hundred ghostly years ago —
That she was Flemish Philip's wife.
  Nor much beyond she cared to know ;
  Without a voice she tells me so.

Philip the Beautiful — whose eyes
  Might win a woman's heart, I fear,
Even from his grave ! " He will arise,"
  The monks had murmured by his bier,
" And reign once more among us here."

She heard their whisper, and forgot
  Castile and Aragon, and all
Save Philip, who had loved her not ;
  The cruel darkness of his pall
  Seemed on an empty world to fall.

She took the dead man — to her sight
  A prince in death's disguise, as fair

As when his wayward smile could light
  The throne he wedded her to share —
  And followed, hardly knowing where.

Almost as dumb as he, she fled,
  Pallid and wasted, toward the place
Where he, the priestly promise said,
  Must wait the hour when God's sweet grace
  Should breathe into his breathless face.

Once, when the night was weird with rain,
  She sought a convent's shelter. When
The tapers showed a veilèd train
  Of nuns, instead of cowlèd men,
  She stole into the night again :

"These women, sainted though they be,"
  She moaned through all her jealous mind,
"Are women still, and shall not see
  Philip the Fair — though he is blind!
  Favor with him I yet shall find."

Then, with her piteous yearning wild:
" Unclose his coffin quick, I pray."
Fiercely the sudden lightning smiled —
When they had laid the lid away —
Like scorn, upon the regal clay.

She kissed the dead of many days,
As though he were an hour asleep.
Dark men with swords to guard her way
Wept for her — but she did not weep;
She had her vigil still to keep.

They reached the appointed cloister. While
The heart of Philip withering lay,
She, without moan, or tear, or smile,
Watched from her window, legends say —
Watched seven-and-forty years away!

Winds blew the blossoms to and fro,
Into the world and out again:

"He will come back to me, I know" —
  Poor whisper of a wandering brain
  To peerless patience, peerless pain.

. . . . Ah, longest, loneliest, saddest tryst
  Was ever kept on earth! And yet
Had he arisen would he have kissed
  The gray wan woman he had met,
  Or — taught her how the dead forget?

Could she have won, discrowned and old,
  The love she could not win, in sooth,
When queenly purple, fold on fold,
  And all the subtle grace of youth,
  Helped her to hide a hapless truth?

Did she not fancy — should she see
  That coffin, watched so long, unclose —
The royal tenant there would be
  Still young, still fair, when he arose,
  Beside her withered leaves and snows?

He would have laughed to breathe the tale
 Of this crazed stranger's love, I fear,
To moon and rose and nightingale,
 With courtly jewels glimmering near,
 Into some lovely lady's ear.

TWO VEILS.

From the nun's wan life a buried passion
Blossomed like a grave-rose in her face ;
" Sweet, my child," she said, " in what fair fashion
Do you mean to wear this lovely lace ?

" Thus ? " — and, with a feverish hand and shaken,
Round her head the precious veil she wound.
" Faith in man," she said, " I have forsaken ;
Faith in God most surely I have found.

" Yet with music in the dewy distance,
And the whole world flowering at my feet,

Through this convent-garment's dark resist-
ance
Backward I can hear my fierce heart beat.

" Tropic eyes too full of light and languor,
Northern soul too gray with Northern frost:
Ashes — ashes after fires of anger !
Love and beauty — what a world I lost ! "

" Sister," laughed the girl with girlish laugh-
ter,
" Sister, do you envy me my veil ? "
" You may come to ask for mine hereafter,"
Answered very piteous lips and pale.

" No, for your black cross is heavy bearing ;
Tiresome counting these stone beads must
be.
Oh, but there are jewels worth the wearing
Waiting in the sunny world for me !

. . . "Sister, have a care — you are forgetting.
Do not broider thorns among my flowers —
Only buds and leaves : your tears are wetting
All my bridal lace." They fell in showers.

After years and years, beside the grating,
(Oh, that saddest sight, young hair grown gray !)
With dry boughs and empty winds awaiting
At the cloister door, came one to pray.

"Sister, see my bride-veil ! there was never
Thorn so sharp as those within its lace.
Sister, give me yours to wear forever ;
Give me yours, and let me hide my face."

TRADITION OF CONQUEST.

His Grace of Marlborough, legends say,
Though battle-lightnings proved his worth,
Was scathed like others, in his day,
By fiercer fires at his own hearth.

The patient chief, thus sadly tried —
Madam, the Duchess, was so fair —
In Blenheim's honors felt less pride
Than in the lady's lovely hair.

Once, (shorn, she had coiled it there to wound
Her lord when he should pass, 'tis said,)
Shining across his path he found
The glory of the woman's head.

No sudden word, nor sullen look,
  In all his after days, confessed
He missed the charm whose absence took
  A scar's pale shape within his breast.

I think she longed to have him blame,
  And soothe him with imperious tears : —
As if her beauty were the same,
  He praised her through his courteous years.

But, when the soldier's arm was dust,
  Among the dead man's treasures, where
He laid it as from moth and rust,
  They found his wayward wife's sweet hair.

TO A DEAD BIRD,

FOUND IN THE WOODS AT EVENING.

Bird of the forest, beautiful and dead!
  While in the twilight here I look on thee,
Strange fancies, of the wild life that has fled,
  Dimly and sadly gather over me,
Until, above thy calm and silent sleep,
I can but bow my aching head and weep.

Alas, that when the Spring-time 's here to wake
  The flowers and music of thy woodland halls,
Thou whose glad voice so sweet a strain could make
  In concert with the winds and water-falls,
In cold and hushed oblivion shouldst lie —
While things that suffer ask, in vain, to die!

But, wast thou purely blest? Ah, who can tell
But birds may have their sorrows? It may be
That boundless love in thy small breast did dwell
For some bright, wingèd thing — that flew from thee
And left his scorn to pierce thy bleeding heart,
Till Death, in pity, drew away its dart!

Or thine, perchance, has been a perfect love,
(If any love can be without a sting!)
And thy lone mate may come to mourn above
Thy blighted beauty, with a drooping wing,
Till, like all lonely mates, he seek relief,
In some new rapture, for his transient grief!

Or thou mayst have been of a royal race;
And radiant throngs of minstrel-things to-day,

Even in thine airy realm's remotest place,
May mourn, or joy, that thou hast passed away, —
For gold and purple glitter on thy breast,
And thou art laid right regally to rest.

Was thy death tranquil? — Or, amid the glare
Of Heaven's fierce fire-arms was thy being sped?
Or did some winged assassin of the air,
For hate, or envy, meet and strike thee dead?
Was life still blushing with youth's rosy glow,
Or, worn and wearied, wast thou glad to go?

And was thy all of joy, or grief, on earth?
Or art thou gone to try thy wing anew
Where lovelier roses have their happier birth,
And woods are ever green, skies ever blue,
And breezy music gushes rich and warm,
With not a sigh, or whisper of the storm?

. . . Fit mausoleum is this hollow tree,
  With faded leaves to pillow thy bright head ;
And, if such rest is all that's left for thee,
  Methinks it is enough, sweet singer dead !
For winds will sing and buds will burst above,
And I 'll believe they left thee here with love !

1857.

MADE OF SHADOW.

THERE is a Picture in the room,
 Somewhere — I only say somewhere.
Cobwebs and dust and subtle gloom
May hide the lips' mysterious bloom
 And that forever-youthful hair.

Whether a thousand years or none
 Have withered since He painted it,
The moon reveals it, and the sun ;
The stars point toward it every one ;
 The shadows show it as they flit.

And was this precious Picture won
 From palace-glimmer over seas ? —
Some king, or else some king's fair son ?

Some soldier whose right arm is done
  With sword and scar? Nay, none of these.

Then by whom painted? — Would you cut
  Into a wound with one sharp word?
The Painter's grave is sealed and shut:
A fairer name than Raphael's — but
  A name that no man ever heard.

Oh, question silence, measure space,
  Or say "I shall be satisfied!" —
But leave that Picture in its place.
We meet each other face to face, —
  We meet, although the world is wide.

I cannot fly the tropic eyes
  Fixed fiercely on my own so long.
They know me through the sad disguise
Of time and sorrow. Tears may rise,
  Imploring them — but they are strong.

. . . . Come, kiss away the Spell, I pray,
  And kiss the beauty I assume,
Sometimes, to match his own, away.
But you must let the Picture stay.
  It is no dream. It is my doom.

IN A QUEEN'S DOMAIN.

Ah, my subject, the rose, I know,
  Will give me her breath and her blush;
And my subject, the lily, spread snow,
  If I pass, for my foot to crush.

My subjects, the lamb and the fawn,
  They hide their heads in my breast;
And my subject, the dove, coos on,
  Though my hand creep close to her nest.

But my subject, the bee, will sting;
  And my subject, the thorn, will tear;
And my subject, the tiger, will spring
  At me, with a cry and a glare.

And my subject, the lion, will shake
  With his anger my loneliest lands;
And my subject, the snake (ah! the snake!)
  Will strike me dead in the sands!

THE SONG NO BIRD SHOULD SING IN VAIN.

THE song no bird should sing in vain,
The song no bird will sing again,
I did not hear before the fleet
Air-singer lost it at my feet.

The wind that blew the enchanted scent
From some divine still continent,
Beat long against my window, but
It found and left my window shut.

The king's fair son, who came in state,
With my lost slipper, for its mate,
I only saw through my regret —
Oh, I am in the ashes yet!

A DEAD MAN'S FRIENDS.

GATHERED from many lands,
  A company still and strange
  In the shadow of velvet and oak! —
  Not one to another spoke.
  With faces that did not change,
Weird with the night and dim,
They were looking their last at him.

If ever men were wise,
  If ever women were fair,
  If ever glory was dust
  In a world of moth and rust, —
  Why these and this were there.
Guests of the great, ah me!
How cold is your courtesy!

Does the loveliest lady of all
  Drop Titian's light from her hair
  Down into his darkened eyes —
  His, who in his coffin lies?
  Does that crouching Venus care
That he must forget the charm
Of her broken, beautiful arm?

Yet these were the dead man's friends,
  Wooed in his passionate youth
  And won when his head was gray; —
  Look at them close, I pray.
  Ah, these he has loved, in sooth;
Yet among them all, I fear,
Is nothing so sweet as — a tear!

MAKING PEACE.

AFTER this feud of yours and mine
The sun will shine ;
After we both forget, forget,
The sun will set.

I pray you think how warm and sweet
The heart can beat ;
I pray you think how soon the rose
From grave-dust grows.

THE BIRD IN THE BRAIN.

In a legend of the East there sits
  A bird with never a mate:
Out of the dead man's brain it flits, —
  Too late for a prayer, too late,
        Repeating all the sin
        Which the beating heart shut in.

Little child of mine, that I kiss and fold,
  With your flower-like hand at my breast,
Already within this head all gold
  That bird is building a nest!
        May it give but one brief cry,
        Sweet, when you come to die.

My lord, the king, that shadowy bird
  Broods under your crown, I fear;

Take care, sir priest, lest you whisper a word
That Heaven were loth to hear: —
Ermine nor lawn will it spare;
Ah, king, ah, priest, take care!

Oh, half-saint sister, so cloister-pale,
That bird will be at your bier.
Though you count your beads, though you wear your veil,
Though you hold your cross right dear,
When your funeral tapers come
Will the weird of wing be dumb?

Poor lover, beware of the bud of the rose
In the maiden's hand at your side:
She has some secret, the dark bird knows,
Which her youth's fair hair can hide;
Turn, maid, from your lover, too —
The bird knows more than you!

SOME RUINED CASTLES.

Come, wailing winds ; come, birds of night ;
  Come, Time, and bring the ivy vine
To wind in constant clasp and bright
  This desolated pride of mine ; —
Come with your mildew and your mold
  For these rich draperies, these fair halls ;
Come with your mosses, and enfold
  These humbled towers, these broken walls !

"A LETTER FROM TO-MORROW."

[THE WORDS OF A CHILD.]

THE child stood sweet and shy:
"Now listen, — do not cry:
'A Letter from To-morrow ——'" he piteously said;
Then wavered, frowned, and blushed,
And looked away and hushed
The elfin voice that spoke through lips of human red.

"I cannot read the rest,"
He prettily confessed,
"Because — it is not plain!" Ah, would I hear it read?

Poor little hands, to hold
A thing so dim and cold,
So full of sad shorn hair and last words of the dead!

Let it go where it will,
There must be news of ill.
Send it to that great house across the shining street: —
To-night, in lights and lace,
There Madam holds her place,
Brief as the foreign flowers that drop dead at her feet.

Madonna-hair and eyes
Remind one of the skies,
(No other picture there more subtly hides its paint.)
Divinely of the earth! —
That last dear dress from Worth
Is too Parisian, perhaps, to fit a saint.

This Letter's shadowy date,
"To-morrow," folds her fate —
(Reach for it, eager arm, so beautiful and bare!)
She reads: "Your hair is gray,
And men forget the day —
Can you remember it? — the day when you were fair!"

He reads — her stately lord,
Out-glittering some chance sword,
Or right new gold, perhaps, wherewith his name was made:
"Taken as in a snare! —
Called by a bird of the air
To justice, go and give and take it, O betrayed!"

Still keep the letter there: —
His boy, the gracious heir

To beauty, love, and hope — a brave enough
estate, —
Lets fall his toys and reads,
"Wounded to death!" and heeds.
A coffin for white flowers stands ready at the
gate.

Give her the letter — see
How fairy-sweet is she,
His girl in her first youth! She droops her
flower-like head,
To read — no charmèd tale
Of bridal buds and vail;
But finds a broken ring and leave to earn her
bread.

Take, now, the letter where
There 's music in the air,
And let the poet read: "The worm likes well
your book."

Painter, if you are he
Master that is to be,
Your name is not in all this Letter, — only look!

Some scented page will bring
This Letter to the king;
To-morrow will be smooth with him and loyal-sweet:
"Your throne is shaken, sire —
Your palace lost in fire;
Your prince must hide with sand the far tracks of his feet!"

Shut close your Letter, child.
The wind is weird and wild —
I give it to the wind to bury in the sea,
Full fathom five, and pray
That till the Judgment Day
No fisherman may bring such treasure up to me!

HER WELL-KNOWN STORY.

She had waited,
On her soft cheek catching many a winter's snow.
Very lovely was the heart unmated ;
Beauty far too beautiful to show,
When her dewy days had withered,
Bloomed below.

Children, brightly,
Near her Christmas windows held their toys and passed ;
Mothers kissed their laughing babies lightly ;
Heads of girls went, sunny-sweet and fast,
Under gifts of bridal blossoms ;
Then, at last,

One green morning,
When small songs were shaking many a pretty
nest,
On her birthday, without any warning,
Came her life-long Lover to her breast,
Bringing white flowers and a casket
Full of rest.

FULFILLMENT.

He who can sing a song more sweet
  Than skylarks learn in finest air,
Hears subtler music at his feet
  Hum in the grass — at his despair.

He who has found a sudden star,
  With new, quick halos for his head,
Sighs for some brighter one afar,
  That sits forever veiled, instead.

He who has dared, though half-afraid,
  To make such beauty of the stone
As God from dust has never made,
  At last looks on it with a moan.

And she who wears such threads of lace
  As fairies might from moonshine spin,
Will find, if any flower she trace,
  The loveliest leaf was not put in.

Yet holds this world one perfect thing,
  That leaves no room to weep or pine ;
You gave it to me with a ring,
  To be forever only mine.

WITH CHILDREN.

THE LITTLE BOY I DREAMED ABOUT.

THIS is the only world I know —
  It is in this same world, no doubt.
Ah me, but I could love him so,
  If I could only find him out, —
  The Little Boy I dreamed about!

This Little Boy, who never takes
  The prettiest orange he can see,
The reddest apple, all the cakes
  (When there are twice enough for three,) —
  Where can the darling ever be?

He does not tease and storm and pout
  To climb the roof in rain or sun,

And pull the pigeon's feathers out
  To see how it will look with none,
  Or fight with hornets one to one!

He does not hide and cut his hair
  And wind the watches wrong, and cry
To throw the kitten down the stair
  And see how often it will die!
  (It 's *strange* that you can wonder why!)

He never wakes too late to know
  A bird is singing near his bed;
He tells the tired moon: "You may go
  To sleep yourself." *He* never said,
  When told to do a thing, "Tell Fred!"

If I say "Go," *he* will not stay
  To lose his hat, or break a toy;
Then hurry like the wind away,

And whistle like the wind, for joy
To please himself — this Little Boy.

Let any stranger come who can,
He will not say — if it *is* true —
"Old Lady" (or "Old Gentleman"),
"I wish you would go home, I do —
I think my mama wants you to!"

No — Fairyland is far and dim:
He does not play in silver sand;
But if I could believe in him
I could believe in Fairyland.
Because —— you do not understand.

Dead — dead? Somehow I do not know.
The sweetest children die. We may
Miss some poor footprint from the snow,
That was his very own to-day.
"God's will" — is what the Christians say.

Like you, or you, or you can be
  When you are good, he looks, no doubt.
I 'd give — the goldenest star I see
  In all the dark to find him out,
  The Little Boy I dreamed about!

THE BABY'S HAND.

What is it the Baby's hand can hold ? —
  Only one little flower, do you say ?
Why, all the blossoms that ever blew
In the sweet wide wind away from the dew,
And all the jewels and all the gold
  Of the kingdoms of the world to-day,
The Baby's hand can hold.

What is it the Baby's hand can hold ?
  Why, all the honey of all the bees,
And all the valleys where summer stays,
And all the sands of the desert's ways,
And all the snows that were ever cold,
  And all the mountains and all the seas,
The Baby's hand can hold.

What is it the Baby's hand can hold —
The Baby's hand so pretty and small?
Why, just what the shoulders of Atlas bear,
Bending him down in the picture there:
(Now all I can tell you is surely told) —
"But that is the world?" Well, that is all
The Baby's hand can hold.

How is it the Baby's hand can hold
The world? —— Yes, surely I ought to know;
For oh, were the Baby's hand withdrawn,
Down into the dust the world were gone,
Folded therein as you might fold
The sad white bud of a rose — just so —
For the Baby's hand to hold.

IF I HAD MADE THE WORLD.

IF I had made the world — ah me!
  I might have left some things undone!
But as to *him* — my boy, you see,
A pretty world this world would be,
  I'd say, without George Washington!

Would I have made the Baby? Oh,
  There were no need of anything
Without the Baby, you must know!
——— I'm a Republican, and so
  I never would have made "the King."

I might have made the President —
  Had I known how to make him right!
——— Columbus? Yes, if I had meant

To find a flowering continent
  Already made for me, I might.

I would have made one poet too —
  Has God made more? ——— Yes, I forgot,
There is no need of asking you;
You know as little as I do.
  A poet is — well, who knows what?

And yet a poet is, my dear,
  A man who writes a book like this,
(There never *was* but one, I hear;)
——— Yes, it is hard to spell S-h-a-k-e-s-p-e-a-r-e.
  So, now, Good-night, — and here 's a kiss.

You are not tired? — you want to know
  What else I would have made? Not much.
A few white lambs that would not grow;

Some violets that would stay ; some snow
  Not quite too cold for you to touch.

I 'd not have taught my birds to fly ;
  My deepest seas would not be deep ! —
My highest mountains hardly high ;
My deserts full of dates should lie —
  But why will you not go to sleep ?

I 'd *not* have made the wind, because
  It 's made of — nothing. Never mind.
Nor any white bears — they have claws ;
(Nor " Science," no, nor " Nature's laws ! ")
  Nor made the North Pole hard to find !

I 'd *not* have made the monkeys — (then
  No one could ever prove to me
There ever was a season when
All these fine creatures we call men
  Hung chattering in some tropic tree !)

Once more, Good-night. This time you
hear?
Please hear as well my morning call.
——— Yes, first I'll tell you something
queer:
If *I* had made the world, I fear—
I'd not have made the world at all!

"MORE ABOUT THE FAIRIES."

In daisy-leaf dresses too pretty to touch,
And little lace-wings made of dreams and of dew,
I think I have told you as much and as much
Of these people of moonshine—as ever I knew!

"Then read about them in the Bible?" Look here,
You smallest of saints (for your first name is Paul),
The truth is, if I can remember, I fear
The Bible says nothing about them at all.

"Then when did God make them?" Why, when he made Eve
They were hid in the lilies of Eden, I guess.
"But the Snake?" — Never mind; you and I will believe
In the angels a little — the snake somewhat less!

You thought it was after the flood they were made
(When the dove was so white and the sea was so dark),
Because there were none of them, you are afraid,
With the other wild animals, saved in the ark!

"But if they are not in the Bible, why then
They are not anywhere — for they cannot be true?"

They're in — next-to-the-Bible! The greatest
of men
Believed in them, surely, as much as you do.

You do *not* believe in them? — "It would be
sin
To believe in things out of the Bible?" Oh,
dear!
Fair sir, are you not rather young to begin
To be doubting the faith of — one Mr.
Shakespeare?

. . . . Still, sooner or later, Time touches the
towers
Where the Golden Hair used to glimmer
so, —
Then what is there left in this wide world of
ours
That we children care any longer to know?

. . . . Go, then, and believe in the red on the rose,
In the gold on the moon, in the butterfly's wings,
And believe, if you will, in — the wind as it blows
The beauty away from all beautiful things!

THE SAD STORY OF A LITTLE GIRL.

Oh, never mind her eyes and hair,
(Though they were dark and it was gold !)
That she was sweet is all I care
To tell you — till the rest is told.
——— " But is the story old ?"

Hush. She *was* sweet ——— Why do I cry ?
Because — her mother loved her so.
I told you that she did not die ;
But she is gone. " Where did she go ? "
Ah me, — I do not know.

" How old was she when she was sweet ? "
Why, one year old, or two, or three.

Here is her shoe — what little feet!
And yet they walked away, you see.
(I must not say, from me.)

"Did Gypsies take her?" Surely, no.
But — something took her; she is lost:
No track of hers in dew or snow,
No heaps of wild buds backward tossed,
To show what paths she crossed.

"Did Fairies take her?" It may be.
For Fairies sometimes, I have read,
Will climb the moonshine, secretly,
To steal a baby from its bed,
And leave an imp instead.

This Changeling, German tales declare,
Make trouble in the house full soon:
Cries at the tangles in its hair,

Beats the piano out of tune,
And — wants to sleep till noon.

And, while it keeps the lost one's face,
It grows less lovely, year by year ——
Yes, in that pretty baby's place
There was a Changeling left, I fear.
. . . . My little maid, do you hear?

AT HANS ANDERSEN'S FUNERAL.

Why, all the children in all the world had list-
ened around his knee,
But the wonder-tales must end ;
So, all the children in all the world came into
the church to see
The still face of their friend.

" But were any fairies there ? " Why, yes, little
questioner of mine,
For the fairies loved him too ;
And all the fairies in all the world, as far as the
moon can shine,
Sobbed, " Oh ! what shall we do ? "

Well, the children who played with the North's
white swans, away in the North's white
snows,
Made wreaths of fir for his head;
And the South's dark children scattered the
scents of the South's red rose
Down at the feet of the dead.

Yes, all the children in all the world were there
with their tears that day;
But the boy who loved him best,
Alone in a damp and lonesome place (not far
from his grave) he lay —
And sadder than all the rest.

"Mother," he moaned, "never mind the king —
why, what if the king is there?
Never mind your faded shawl:
The king may never see it; for the king will
hardly care
To look at your clothes at all."

So, close to his coffin she crouched, in the
breath of the burial flowers,
And begged for a bud or a leaf :—
"If I cannot have one, O sirs, to take to that
poor little room of ours,
My boy will die of his grief!"

My child, if the king *was* there, and I think he
was (but then I forget),
Why, that was a little thing.
Did a dead man ever lift his head from its place
in the coffin yet,
Do you think, to bow to the king?

"But could he not see him up in Heaven?" I
never was there, you know;
But Heaven is too far, I fear,
For the ermine, and purple, and gold, that make
up the king, to show
So bravely as they do here.

But he saw the tears of the peasant-child, by
the beautiful light he took
From the earth in his close-shut eyes ;
For tears are the sweetest of all the things we
shall see, when we come to look
From the windows of the skies.

WISHING FOR DIAMONDS.[1]

DIAMONDS? Ah, me! I 've heard of some
  That you might have. Yes, I know where.
A princess wore them. She is dumb,
  And deaf, and blind. She will not care.

"What does she wear without them?" Oh,
  White linen, folded. That is best.
If you were she? — you would not know,
  Perhaps, how sweetly you were dressed.

"Where are the diamonds?" In the East
  A king sits grieving so, to-day,
That neither soldier, slave, nor priest
  Dare speak to him, the whispers say.

[1] The allusions in this piece are to a newspaper account of, with the circumstances attending, the death of a daughter of the Khedive of Egypt.

You did not know that there were things
  In all this world, or any place,
That ever *could* be hard for kings ? —
  His trouble makes him hide his face.

" Then is his palace lost ? " Why, no ;
  Not lost, but empty — that is it.
The enchanted lamps above him glow ;
  The satin shadows round him flit.

Meanwhile his camels wander by,
  The poor get gold and wine and bread ;
And Egypt hears the old, old cry,
  Because his favorite child is dead.

. . . . It is the diamonds — I forget ?
  You wonder where they can be hid ?
I fear that you could see them yet ;
  They are upon her coffin lid.

Something the princess there has not,
  Something you have, would buy them quite
A thousand times. What is it, what ? —
  Then you would give it, if you might ?

. . . . Ah, what is bitter, what is true,
  In this sweet, doubtful world but death ?
. . . . So you will give it, will you — you ?
  Well, then, red lips, it is your breath.

VOICES OF THE NIGHT.

(*Sung to a Wakeful Little Boy one Rainy Autumn Evening.*)

Good Little Boy, have you got any fire,
To warm a little fairy
Wet and dripping,
Out-doors knocking ? —
Good Little Boy, have you got any fire ?

Good Little Boy, have you got any fire,
To warm a little puppy,
Wet and dripping,
Out-doors barking ? —
Good Little Boy, have you got any fire ?

Good Little Boy, have you got any fire,
To warm a little kitten,
Wet and dripping,
Out-doors mewing? —
Good Little Boy, have you got any fire?

Good Little Boy, have you got any fire,
To warm a little fairy,
Wet and dripping,
Out-doors knocking? —
Good Little Boy, have you got any fire?

1865.

www.ingramcontent.com/pod-product-compliance
Lightning Source LLC
LaVergne TN
LVHW021420110826
845150LV00007B/2005

* 9 7 8 1 4 2 5 5 0 8 7 2 2 *